# THROUGH
## THEIR EYES

### IN OTHER WORDS

Edited By Machaela Gavaghan

First published in Great Britain in 2020 by:

Young Writers
Remus House
Coltsfoot Drive
Peterborough
PE2 9BF
Telephone: 01733 890066
Website: www.youngwriters.co.uk

All Rights Reserved
Book Design by Ashley Janson
© Copyright Contributors 2019
Softback ISBN 978-1-83928-717-6

Printed and bound in the UK by BookPrintingUK
Website: www.bookprintinguk.com
YB0430Z

# FOREWORD

Since 1991, here at Young Writers we have celebrated the awesome power of creative writing, especially in young adults, where it can serve as a vital method of expressing strong (and sometimes difficult) emotions, a conduit to develop empathy, and a safe, non-judgemental place to explore one's own place in the world. With every poem we see the effort and thought that each pupil published in this book has put into their work and by creating this anthology we hope to encourage them further with the ultimate goal of sparking a life-long love of writing.

*Through Their Eyes* challenged young writers to open their minds and pen bold, powerful poems from the points-of-view of any person or concept they could imagine – from celebrities and politicians to animals and inanimate objects, or even just to give us a glimpse of the world as they experience it. The result is this fierce collection of poetry that by turns questions injustice, imagines the innermost thoughts of influential figures or simply has fun.

The nature of the topic means that contentious or controversial figures may have been chosen as the narrators, and as such some poems may contain views or thoughts that, although may represent those of the person being written about, by no means reflect the opinions or feelings of either the author or us here at Young Writers.

We encourage young writers to express themselves and address subjects that matter to them, which sometimes means writing about sensitive or difficult topics. If you have been affected by any issues raised in this book, details on where to find help can be found at *www.youngwriters.co.uk/info/other/contact-lines*

# CONTENTS

**Harris Girls' Academy East Dulwich, Southwark**

| | |
|---|---|
| Fatimatu Bah (12) | 1 |
| Anabel Ezinne Nwankwo (13) | 2 |
| Rakeb Zewde (12) | 4 |
| Guinevere Cooper (11) & Amilah Ahmed-Dobson | 6 |
| Belen Justiniano Roca (16) | 8 |
| Lillie Stanhope (13) | 10 |
| Awele Sharon Emeka-Benokwu (13) | 11 |
| Amelie Buci (12) | 12 |
| Fahridat Badmus (12) | 13 |
| Lola David (12) | 14 |
| Jada Flora D'Ambrosio (12) | 15 |
| Leyla Rafiou (13) | 16 |
| Stephanie Nofiu (11) | 17 |
| Michelle John-Okoro (11) | 18 |
| Mandy Pokuaa Badu (12) | 19 |
| Mehdia Zaidi Syeda (14) | 20 |
| Janet Kuseju (13) | 21 |
| Rashida Martins (13) | 22 |
| Iasmyn de Oliveira Rego Linhares (13) | 23 |
| Ivy Salter-Chiles (11) | 24 |
| Fathia O. Kolawole (11) | 25 |
| Jadesola Elizabeth Oyenuga (13) | 26 |
| Hawa Bangura (13) | 27 |
| Nyla Brinae McPherson (12) | 28 |
| Jia Hui Zhou (13) | 29 |
| Victoria Amako (12) | 30 |
| Bethany Grace Black (13) | 31 |

**Largs Academy, Largs**

| | |
|---|---|
| Ruby Rose Anderson (12) | 32 |
| Ailidh Brobyn (12) | 34 |
| Lucy Cairns (12) | 36 |
| Ellis Dixon (11) | 38 |
| James Millar (12) | 39 |
| Isla Waller (12) | 40 |
| Hope Kitty Phillips (12) | 42 |
| Naideen Dailly (11) | 43 |
| September Lillie McKee (12) | 44 |
| Jessica MacCalman (12) | 45 |
| Josh Gilmour (11) | 46 |
| Rohan Meechan (12) | 47 |
| Scarlett Walker (12) | 48 |
| Kate Maccalman (12) | 49 |
| Jessica Helen Langdon (11) | 50 |
| Callum Stewart (11) | 51 |
| Jackson Burleigh (11) | 52 |
| Emma Mattheessens (12) | 53 |
| Noah Graham (12) | 54 |
| Cameron Samuel Greenham (11) | 55 |
| Cara Russell (11) | 56 |
| Ellie Smith (11) | 57 |
| Ophelia Charlotte Elizabeth McNeill Conner (12) | 58 |
| Fraser Angus MacLean Waters (12) | 59 |
| Hannah McNicol (12) | 60 |
| Strath Ferguson (12) | 61 |
| Rhys Joshua Franchetti (12) | 62 |
| Ava Miriam Barbour-Weatherill (11) | 63 |
| Cooper Wark (12) | 64 |
| Frederick L F Smith (12) | 65 |
| Ruaridh Wightman (12) | 66 |
| Victoria Cox (11) | 67 |

| | |
|---|---|
| Freya MacArthur (12) | 68 |
| Rowan Guthrie Roberts (12) | 69 |
| Nitcha McLaughlin (11) | 70 |

## St Thomas More Catholic School, Bedford

| | |
|---|---|
| Seif Elbadry (12) | 71 |
| Jessica Abisola Samuel (11) | 72 |
| Oisin Baird (11) | 73 |
| Eleanor Dutton (11) | 74 |
| Ryan Ythan Grobates Apolinario (11) | 75 |
| Luca Scozzari (11), Antonio Donny Bosco & Fintan Horsman | 76 |
| Lorenzo-Dane Dipasupil (12) | 77 |
| Marley Bulzis (11) | 78 |
| Pablo Dy (12) | 79 |
| Shaun Osasu Osaghae (12) | 80 |
| Magda Pernisco (11) | 81 |
| Orlagh Louise Brunning (11) | 82 |
| Honey-Leigh Williams (13) | 83 |
| Molly Bedingfield (11) | 84 |
| Wojciech Bronakowski (11) | 85 |
| Shaun Marsh (11) | 86 |
| Simren Kaur (12) | 87 |
| Sama Mohamed Saeed Ali (11) | 88 |
| Harvey Chiarn (11) | 89 |
| Leo Valentine Barker (11) | 90 |
| Bryan Chanpda (11) | 91 |
| Iggy Shanthakumar (11) | 92 |
| Max Ellis Owen (12) | 93 |
| Nancy Finn (11) | 94 |
| Rebecca (12) & Victoria Jelisaveta Kaczalek | 95 |
| Sophia Hope Witton (11) | 96 |
| Alex Silva (11) | 97 |
| David Hallsworth (11) | 98 |
| Johnny Farmer (11) | 99 |
| Szymon Jedrzejewski (11) | 100 |
| Fin Crofts (11) | 101 |
| Alexander Gallagher (11) | 102 |

## The Matthew Arnold School, Staines Upon Thames

| | |
|---|---|
| Hushmeet Singh Nagpal (11) | 103 |
| Laura Valentina Mantilla (14) | 104 |
| Kacey Rice (13) | 106 |
| Nicolly Victoria Jeronimo (16) | 107 |
| Emma Jones (13) | 108 |
| Krrish Parajiya (15) | 109 |
| Jack Barber (15) | 110 |
| Rachel Jimenez (13) | 111 |
| Alex Jennings (15) | 112 |
| Laine Beacham (13) | 113 |
| Grace Ager (15) | 114 |
| Luca Saftoiu (11) | 115 |
| Sarah Abusaid (11) | 116 |
| Luke Francis (13) | 117 |
| Alfie Bailey (15) | 118 |
| Mathew Foster (15) | 119 |
| George Bignell (13) | 120 |
| Oliver Long (11) | 121 |
| Louis Reed (15) | 122 |
| Heston Charles Reed (15) | 123 |

## Upton Hall School FCJ, Upton

| | |
|---|---|
| Summer Henning (12) | 124 |
| Ava Langley (11) | 126 |
| Hannah Brearton (11) | 128 |
| Bethany Addenbrooke (11) | 130 |
| Emily Grace Lowry-Bartram (11) | 132 |
| Annelie Wheeler (11) | 134 |
| Karen Kiama (12) | 135 |
| Emma Harrison (12) | 136 |
| Sasha Ratchford (11) | 138 |
| Mollie Wilson (12) | 139 |
| Phoebe Ferguson (13) | 140 |
| Amelia Hennell (12) | 141 |
| Lucy Turner (12) | 142 |
| Neve Piercy (11) | 143 |
| Imogen Hunt (11) | 144 |
| Mia Annabel Waring-Jones (12) | 145 |
| Lucy Birtwistle (11) | 146 |
| Emily May Jackson (11) | 147 |

| | |
|---|---|
| Madelyn McGreevy (12) | 148 |
| Dakota Drake (12) | 149 |
| Amy Mair Flanders (12) | 150 |
| Hollie Cowen (13) | 151 |
| Rowan Swale-Beswick (11) | 152 |
| Lili-Louise Amis (11) | 153 |
| Mae Evie Hodgers (12) | 154 |
| Anna Ryan (12) | 155 |
| Millie Ellen Newton (11) | 156 |
| Gia Hothersall (13) | 157 |
| Grace Stella Harvey (11) | 158 |
| Evelyn Gallon (12) | 159 |
| Lara Corcoran (11) | 160 |
| Rosie Beamish (12) | 161 |
| Faye Simpson (11) | 162 |
| Harriet Andrews (12) | 163 |
| Kate Farmer (12) | 164 |

# THE
# POEMS

## My Colour, Me

I am black, not white,
Does it hurt you that I'm a different colour to you
Because I'm dark, not light?
Is it you can't see the beauty in black,
You only see it in white?
Does it make a difference
Because black isn't on the rainbow?
I have to separate from white people in the toilets
Because my blackness will stain the pearl-white toilet.
There are stereotypes of black people,
But not one about white people,
Us black people are beautiful inside,
Although you might not see it,
But we all have beauty inside.
Our ancestors had to go through so much pain:
Beatings, whippings, branding,
Are you trying to bring that back?
Do you like to see us suffer?
You say we're unattractive, but you act like us,
You think it's okay to say the N word,
That word was used to put us down
But now we'll use it to bring us up.

**Fatimatu Bah (12)**
Harris Girls' Academy East Dulwich, Southwark

# The Power Of Time

"Who is the greatest ruler?" you ask
And yet, without knowing, we are all its subjects
Its immortality enslaving us into a life of misery and death
The monotonous journey that is life
And yet you ask
"Who is the greatest ruler?"

For it has the power
To use centuries, decades, years, months
Wars, violence, fighting, bloodshed
To find peace, without actually finding peace at all
But instead passing on the anxieties of today
To trouble a future generation
And ignorantly wasting away the precious, indispensable gift
It, our ruler, has gifted us all with
The clock ticking away before your very eyes.

"What gift have we been gifted?" you ask
While our ruler is, at this moment
Mercilessly seizing it, that very gift, from millions
And you, despite living in this same world
And breathing the same air
Waste away the minutes, and yet you ask
"What gift have we been gifted?"

Until the moment is taken away from you
And you are left shaking on your deathbed

Begging for our ruler to show mercy on you
Longing for another chance
But instead, the clock is ticking away before your very eyes
As they close in preparation for the distressing events to come
And yet you asked, "Where has the time gone?"

**Anabel Ezinne Nwankwo (13)**
Harris Girls' Academy East Dulwich, Southwark

# Yes I'm Black, So What?

Yes, I'm black and I'm back
I'll say it out loud
I am from Ethiopia
I have all the reason to be proud
So I'm gonna walk with a smile on my face
Praying one day you'll stop discriminating my race.

Yes, I'm black and I'm back
As I'm ready to roll
Ethiopia and England are my home sweet home
As the cross on my neck defines me
I'm an Ethiopian Orthodox, all of my family.

As an Ethiopian, we have a beautiful culture
We are taught to respect humankind
And our Mother Nature.

I will stand up tall with pride
For who I am
Just remember, it doesn't cost a penny to be kind.

So if you know
Let your hatred go
We are equal like the colours in the rainbow
Even if our race contrasts
We have more in common than we think.

So I'm gonna say it one more time
Don't break this line

'Cause this phrase is mine
Yes, I'm black, so what?

## Rakeb Zewde (12)
Harris Girls' Academy East Dulwich, Southwark

# Occupation

Many people come and go
Why they do, I do not know
Soldiers here always stay
They're always here, every day

They're in hospital
All of my friends
The pain and suffering
It never ends

Even with the help we get
The war won't stop; it's not done yet
The men with guns, they fight us hard
They leave every man scarred.

The air I breathe is full of fear
There isn't a single brave one left here
For 102 years this has been
You have no clue what I've seen.

You call us terrorists
Yet you are the terrorisers
Nothing will ever hold you back
For you relentlessly attack.

You occupy our homes
And you throw sticks and stones
My people are misunderstood
So you terrorise our neighbourhoods.

Your gases and guns
Destroying my lungs
All because I come from Palestine.

**Guinevere Cooper (11) & Amilah Ahmed-Dobson**
Harris Girls' Academy East Dulwich, Southwark

# Will I See You?

I remember my first day at school
Entering the classroom
And heading straight to the back table
And right there
Is where I found you.

You said something
I smiled
At that moment, I knew
I would see you every day
And I was certain
You knew that too.

Your laugh was always present
Even when you fell and tripped
You laughed, hiding the pain
And even now I wish
I could laugh like you did
Whenever I remember you.

I never knew when you left
Until one day
You were gone
And that night
I held the pink teddy
That you gave me.

And if one day I were to see you
I can picture you shouting my name
Arms waving like a crazy squid
And me turning back
Certain that it is none other than you
Because only you...
Would laugh like that.

## Belen Justiniano Roca (16)
Harris Girls' Academy East Dulwich, Southwark

# Choosing My Future

It is stress
It is panic
For a couple of years, it's pure pressure
It is all you think about
It is your future
It tells us to 'make the right choice'
But we don't know what that is yet
Parents, teachers, friends and family
Tell you to pick wisely
When I think about choosing my options
All I see is turquoise
It cannot pick between blue and green
Just like I cannot pick between geography and history
It is always there in the back of your mind
From the second you start Year 7
To the moment you leave in Year 11
You will ask yourself, *what will I choose?*
Then ask yourself, *did I choose right?*
But this pressure is on all of us
Children, teenagers, Years 7s, 8s, 9s, 10s and 11s
We all choose our future as kids.

**Lillie Stanhope (13)**
Harris Girls' Academy East Dulwich, Southwark

# Judgement

Drums bang continuously
Flashing neon red
The hurricane that disrupts my mind
The hurtful words that are released from people's mouths disgust me
People snigger and stare
It is torture.

It is the frustration that runs inside of me
The menacing deep voice stalks me
The claustrophobic feeling
The wondering eyes and stares.

It is not hilarious
It is not generous or delightful
It is the image of segregation
The curiosity
You claim you want equality
But judge people of different races.

It is hypocritical
It is disrespectful
It burns my organs inside
Why can't I glorify and praise my friends without being judged?
It is not right
And I really won't give up without a fight.

## Awele Sharon Emeka-Benokwu (13)
Harris Girls' Academy East Dulwich, Southwark

# The Truth About Sexism

It is the colour pink
It is the colour blue
It is not green or yellow
It is the separation of people just because they're not the same
Because they're not all like you.

It is like a piano
A piano that doesn't make any sound
No matter how hard you play
Nothing comes out.

It is not an ice cream
It is a chilling voice
Telling you what you can't do because of your gender
Telling you what you have to do because of your gender.

It is a cage
That all girls in the world are trapped in
And all of 'mankind' is working to keep that cage locked.

It is the colour pink that separates us
It is also the colour blue.

It is a closed book
With no cover.

**Amelie Buci (12)**
Harris Girls' Academy East Dulwich, Southwark

# Destiny

This subject, racism, has taken thousands to their deaths
Like the chugging of the train on the track
With people on board who will never come back;
Auschwitz.

Just because one race is the majority
And others are the minority
It doesn't make you superior
Stop making us feel inferior.

We look back to the hundreds of years of slavery
Not just was it that
It was hundreds of years of bravery.

We are all mankind
We might not think the same
Or have the same mind
It's time to grow up
And put our differences behind.

We are the new generation
We need peace and a moment of meditation
It is for you and me
And up to us to make our destiny.

**Fahridat Badmus (12)**
Harris Girls' Academy East Dulwich, Southwark

# Climate Change

It is the cello with only one string
Its colour is a clouded, unclear grey
The weather it causes is indecisive
Chopping and changing from tranquil to chaos
It is the neglected, musty jumper
At the back of your wardrobe, wasting away to nothing
It's screaming for help in a dark room with a torturer in hot pursuit
Its voice has cracked from repeating the same message for too long
Its volume is slowly but surely dying, too tired to speak no more
I feel an immense sorrow towards it
Yet frustration towards those who ignored its first cries of desperation
Its emotion is a mixture of anger and fear
If it were an image, it would be a funeral
With people crying, wishing they could change the past.

**Lola David (12)**
Harris Girls' Academy East Dulwich, Southwark

## Animal Cruelty

It is the colour black,
Shutting yourself from nature,
Locking yourself in an underground cellar,
Away from the reach of light and sound,
Away from the world,
In an instance, it's done,
You've killed an animal,
With no feeling of sorrow,
Ignorance,
It controls,
Like a puppet master controlling a puppet,
Deciding its every move and word,
All those innocent animals,
Gone,
We kill them for their meat,
We kill them for their skin,
We kill them for their tusks,
But what do they do to us?
Nothing.
Since us humans have come into existence,
Animals are disappearing before our eyes,
But we are trying to cover up the truth with lies.

**Jada Flora D'Ambrosio (12)**
Harris Girls' Academy East Dulwich, Southwark

# Rivalry

It is the big trumpet,
It is not the small clarinet,
It is the colour black,
Unseeable yet still present.

It is the bitterness of winter,
It is not the warmness of summer,
It shouts from the top of its lungs,
It doesn't whisper.

Its voice is graspy and rough,
Not soft and smooth,
It is loud and inevitable,
It is not quiet and unnoticeable.

It is the selfishness of our today,
Not the selflessness of our yesterday,
Nothing is worth more than the happiness in your heart,
But yet it shows the anger.

It is the world crumbling to pieces,
It is not the world coming together.

## Leyla Rafiou (13)
Harris Girls' Academy East Dulwich, Southwark

# Cancer

I am a destroyed, isolated, not-cared-for piano
That plays in the dark my dreadful song
Every second, every moment.

If I were a colour, I would be red for blood,
Vital fluids and medicine.

If I were a type of weather,
I would be a hurricane
Because I leave destruction and fear.

If I were a piece of clothing,
I would be a hat
Because I am always on your mind.

If I were going to say something,
I would say I don't care about you
Over and over again.

I am like nails running down a chalkboard.

Sorrow.
Burning all your desire.
Hope.
Flat on the floor.

## Stephanie Nofiu (11)
Harris Girls' Academy East Dulwich, Southwark

# Climate Change

It is the colour blue
Blue for all the waves full of plastic
And the smoke we feed the sky
Every day
The sky silently whispers, "Stop, stop, please listen!
The poison hurts, the smoke you feed me."

The endless cries sound like two hollow pots
The careless way that people are treating this planet
It makes me feel outraged and annoyed
People are not taking this seriously
Does anyone ever listen?

Whatever we do to our planet affects us too
If you try to destroy it, it will destroy you
The world cries in pain
But nobody bothers
Nobody cares
Nobody listens.

**Michelle John-Okoro (11)**
Harris Girls' Academy East Dulwich, Southwark

# Assumptions

It is the colour red
Every time I am humiliated about walking with my brother
Why?
Because you make assumptions about who we are
The sounds are two blocked flutes in my ears.

I have a voice, a shaky voice, wanting to shout 'stop'
It is assumptions about who we are
Our personality, ethnicity or religion
It is the person who walks out every day
And hears rumours about who she is.

It is the colour red
The girl you made gloomy is still depressed
Have you thought about the girl you took everything from?
Assumptions only become worse.

### Mandy Pokuaa Badu (12)
Harris Girls' Academy East Dulwich, Southwark

# Insomniac

If he were a musical instrument
He would be a non-stopping triangle,
For the triangle imitates his brother
The ticks of time.
He lives as fire and water
Red and blue
Purple.
He lurks,
Like the everlasting daylight in the poles.

He is flesh, not clothing
He is a part of you
His presence silently lingers behind you
He haunts you, yet it's somewhat comforting.

He shall *remain*.

He brings questions
He brings war
He brings insomniacs
Repels euphoriacs.

He is Insomnia
I am his slave.

## Mehdia Zaidi Syeda (14)
Harris Girls' Academy East Dulwich, Southwark

# Money

It has no specific colour
Yet it brings such happiness or doom
And it drives us to every extent
Because we are ever so consumed

Money

We revolve around such signs
Which seem to manipulate our every decision
But how could it be meaningless to me
Without being important to you?

Money

Do you ever think of a world
Where money isn't all alpha
Where cost hasn't evolved
Where there is a happily ever after.

Money

When will we be able to realise
The power of money has taken us all?

## Janet Kuseju (13)
Harris Girls' Academy East Dulwich, Southwark

# The Needle

Molten tears streaking down his face,
Broken screams ripping through the silence,
Was this retribution
For his ignorant defiance?

Her laughs rang through his mind,
Dulcet and pious,
Was this all it would take
For the young boy's compliance?

Hazy memories resurfaced in his head
Of all the young boys he knew,
But for what did it matter?
They were all long-gone and dead.

As the needle tore into his skin,
Her voice grew quiet,
Was this his eternal punishment
Or a chance to finally meet his kin?

**Rashida Martins (13)**
Harris Girls' Academy East Dulwich, Southwark

# I'm Going Home

Hearing the volume rising, my heart racing
Upbeat music making my palms sweat
My belly flip
The sweet voice that blasts from the radio
She sings so softly, yet with so much passion
Bolsa nova it is
It is the colour yellow and green
It is hot and wet
Making my cheeks flush pink
It means that the family is united once again
However, it is now quiet
It is now storming
It is now grey and lifeless
And the only sound I hear
Is the clock ticking on the wall
*Tick-tock, tick-tock...*

**Iasmyn de Oliveira Rego Linhares (13)**
Harris Girls' Academy East Dulwich, Southwark

# Global Warming

I see a polar bear desperately trying to keep afloat on a melting iceberg.

I hear the screaming of dying animals in the Amazon rainforest.

I smell the wood smoke of millions of trees in flames;
Their leaves blistering.

I touch the salty seawater as it overflows into people's homes.

I taste the foulness of pollution in the air around me.

I watch the world falling apart around me.
Will this global torture ever end?

**Ivy Salter-Chiles (11)**
Harris Girls' Academy East Dulwich, Southwark

# Differences

It's painful
It's torturing
It's like getting stabbed in the heart
It's like you're not wanted
It's like somebody calling you what you are not
This needs to stop
*Differences are shown*
We are being harassed 'cause we are black
We are treated differently 'cause we are black
The apartheid was based on *us!*

Our voices need to be heard
We need to stand up for our human rights!

## Fathia O. Kolawole (11)
Harris Girls' Academy East Dulwich, Southwark

# Low Self-Esteem

It is the colour white
It is a flute struggling to get its soulful sound out
It is motionless
It is a fuzzy scarf being placed around your neck with no reference
No protection; just silence
It is a fly swarming for food
But eventually getting killed
It isn't the colour gold, nor silver
It has sharp edges but smooth sides
Six faces but one side
It has a heart
Which beats every time it hears a rhythmic song.

**Jadesola Elizabeth Oyenuga (13)**
Harris Girls' Academy East Dulwich, Southwark

# Her

Power to some is weapons,
Power to some is knowledge,
Power to some is control,
Power to some is education,
But she never took advantage of her power.

And that was the special thing about her,
She never gave up on anything,
Even with the voices in her head,
Telling her that she wasn't worth it,
She never let it get in the way,
Determined,
A fighter,
A leader,
Not by chance, but at heart.

### Hawa Bangura (13)
Harris Girls' Academy East Dulwich, Southwark

# Why?

I don't understand
Why people are split
Is it an idea, a game
Does anyone win?

I don't understand with people go bad
They corrupt, they break, but inside
Are they sad?

I don't understand why people are killed
I know why
But why should their blood be spilled?

I don't understand how knowledge is power
When questions are out there
Waiting to be answered.

### Nyla Brinae McPherson (12)
Harris Girls' Academy East Dulwich, Southwark

# Still

Underneath the dark grey skies
A lone man waits until he dies
The laughter of rifles echoes through the trees
Bringing every living thing down to their knees

The breeze of power changes with time
From him to him to him
It is not a stationary thing
Paying the world with sin.

### Jia Hui Zhou (13)
Harris Girls' Academy East Dulwich, Southwark

# She Is Pretty

She is pretty, but not like the models you see on Instagram
She is pretty for her warm and loving heart
She is pretty for how she looks on the inside, not out
She is not pretty for how her hair looks or what she wears

She is pretty for who she is.

**Victoria Amako (12)**
Harris Girls' Academy East Dulwich, Southwark

# Failure

One sheet of paper
Determines your whole life
If that sheet doesn't bring joy
It brings judgement and fear
Yet there is nothing you can do about it.

Dreams are crushed
Confidence drops
You're now considered
A failure.

**Bethany Grace Black (13)**
Harris Girls' Academy East Dulwich, Southwark

# My Cat, Thomas

I wake you up, out of your sleep
I jump and leap upon your bed
For I want my early morning food
For I know that I've been good

I love to snooze
But if you wake me, you'll lose
I'll spread my fluff all over your house
I'll catch you a bird or even a mouse

I might claw or scratch you if you annoy me
But when I want to be fed, I'm like a bee
I love when you scratch under my chin
I'll stretch out and give you a grin

I love outside to run through the grass
And sleep in the sun
I find it rather quite fun
Although I'm very lazy so I might not run

I love my owner, although it might not show
Out of cats and dogs, my bar is pretty low
For more people love dogs
But I am better than those ghastly hogs

You don't have to take me for a walk
And if I want food, I'll meow, not talk
You don't have to throw me a ball
And if I may fall, I will land on four feet

I'm elegant, even when I eat
I stand tall when I walk down the street
I'll come and curl up on your lap
Or even lie on you when you have a nap

Don't go buy those cute little puppies
Come buy us kittens
With little white mittens.

## Ruby Rose Anderson (12)
Largs Academy, Largs

# Escaping War

*Bang!*
I shudder with fear
Dad once said, "War brings only sadness."
Another bang
And I can barely hear
In the quick of a flash
Mum comes to a conclusion
We must run from this place that I call home
She says, "No bags!" and that's her final decision
We run for the door, then onto a boat
And I wave goodbye to my only home.

I look around, for somewhere to run
Then Mum notices a cupboard on the boat
She says there's only space for one
She helps me in and closes the door
Then I hear a voice
I'm scared so I hold my breath
And refuse to make a noise.

After hours of silence
I hear the arrival bell
I hear a click, then off goes a gun
Then I'm even more scared as I hear someone yell
When all the chaos is over
I run from the boat
Then hide from the business

And cry by the moat
With no mum or dad
Until I see a camp.

Now that I'm safe
I refuse to be sad
Though tough times are hard
This could be a new start.

### Ailidh Brobyn (12)
Largs Academy, Largs

# The Little Kitty

Out the door, there they fled,
Left me here, barely fed,
Off to work, off to school,
I am scared of the dirty pool...

As I crawl by, I slip,
But why? I am as small as a mince pie,
Now I might die, drowning as I cry,
I see a light and with all my might, I struggle
And squirm until I get a grip as firm as stone
On a dead bird's bone.

As I gasp for breath with all I have left,
I hear the car pull up,
Then I hear a click,
I meow in fear as I hear her come near,
She asks why the carpet is wet,
I look at her with regret,
*Crash! Bang!*
She has just chipped my little fang,
I whimper in pain,
She throws me so high,
I feel like I can touch the sky,
I land on my head,
I feel like I'm going to be dead...

But I'm not, I am escaping,
I can see the back window open, gaping,
Hooray, I have fled, now to find a comfy bed!

## Lucy Cairns (12)
Largs Academy, Largs

# Pumpkin Catastrophies

Here I sit, inside a shop
Hoping I don't get picked up
I'm watching the sky as the raindrops fall
What a nice play to be in the mall

As somebody brings me home
I get placed on the kitchen counter
My owner runs a bath and it starts to foam
I just want to get away from here and my founder

They pull out knives to carve me in
They take out everything inside me and chuck it in the bin
As they cut the top off of me
I scream, but nobody can hear me

I now have a face, but a very angry one
I'm sitting out on the patio in the freezing cold
Now I am getting very cold
And that's not good because I'm getting old

Now it's time, Halloween is over
If only I could find a four-leaf clover
Maybe then I could still be alive.

## Ellis Dixon (11)
Largs Academy, Largs

# Money

I am printed out of the factory
I am ready to begin my journey
Handed out to a child
And spent on sweets
Then into a register
Taken out, given to an old lady
Then she gives me to her grandchild
He shows me to his friend
"Wow!"
Then I'm taken to school to show off
But I am taken by the school bully
Then given to his mum to pay the house debt
I watch them get evicted
Now I'm in the hands of a businessman
I'm in a photocopier
Being used to print *fake* money
Now caught by the police
I was taken to the bank
A bomb went off
The bank was being bombarded and robbed
Now I'm back in the hands of criminals.

**James Millar (12)**
Largs Academy, Largs

# Peace, That's All I Want

I'm a Scottish evacuee
My home is Clydebank
But now I live in Wales
My home was bombed
So I was given a new one
Miles away from my mother

I cried on the train
I cry in my bed
I cry whenever Lynne's not here
Lynne is my new mum, who's not very nice
She makes me work hard
All day on the farm

In my dreams
I dream of Scotland
Getting destroyed
I dream of my mother
And that she is dead
I wake up screaming
Lynne comes to my bed and shouts
"Well if you're awake then let's get to work!"

I don't like it here
I never will
Peace
That's all I want

Love
That's all I need.

## Isla Waller (12)
Largs Academy, Largs

# The Loving Dog

I am called Charles and I am a loving, sweet dog
I loved my owner so much

My owner was a funny and happy boy
But he just went to college without me
He left me with his parents

His parents don't pay any attention to me
They only feed me!

I love my owner, I want him to come back
It's been two years since I saw him last

But yesterday his parents took me on a walk
I was super excited
But they took me to the park
They left me there...

It was the day my owner was supposed to arrive home
All of a sudden, I looked up
He was standing in front of me
He took me home
And he played games with me.

**Hope Kitty Phillips (12)**
Largs Academy, Largs

# An Alien Trying To Save Earth

All around me is confusion
But I know what I must do
Can we reverse the damage?
Do they understand me?
Everything is weird
Far and wide are people
Going on their way
Hopefully I can help them
I know I must try
Jupiter is where I'm from
Keep on trying, keep on working
Losing this unfair war
Make a change now
No one even cares
Offer a hand
Please stop this
Question us no more
Recycle your plastic
Stop killing your planet
To understand you must listen
Use this knowledge
Verses pollution in this war
Where am I?
Xenon is tiny, like pollution should be
You can help
Zebras must be saved!

**Naideen Dailly (11)**
Largs Academy, Largs

# The Night, So Lonely

After night has fallen,
Before the sun rises,
Cat sits down so lonely,
Defeated by loneliness,
Every night is the same,
Forever the same,
Getting to be a habit,
Hoping they wake up,
In their beds asleep,
Joining in the chorus,
Keep going until morning,
Leaving food isn't enough,
Making a friendship isn't enough,
Never playing with me,
Other humans coming in
Pretend to love me,
Questions that don't have answers,
Resting your head on the pillow,
Strutting into the room,
Trying to wake you up,
Under the bed I go,
When will you wake up and give me food?

## September Lillie McKee (12)
Largs Academy, Largs

# A Day In The Life Of Breac

I'll start my day by waking you up
Licking your face, jumping upon your bed
For I want my breakfast
I want to go for a walk
To chase the squirrels.

I'll snooze all day
Although if you awaken me
I shall not talk to you for the rest of the day!

I will bark if you walk by my house
I will wait and wait all day long
Until you appear out of the blue.

There she is!
She's coming, she's coming
Get the ball, get the ball,
She's coming!

Will she find out that I chewed the letter?
Will she? Will she?

Oh no...
She did!

### Jessica MacCalman (12)
Largs Academy, Largs

# Woody The Dog

Woody
Who is hilarious, daft and sporty
Who is the big brother of Marco and Patricia
Who loves bones, football and running
Who feels ecstatic, excited and hyper
Who needs love, to be cared for, taken for walks
Who gives gifts, fun and ginormous cuddles
Who fears bigger and badder dogs and cats
Who would like to see Kilmarnock FC win the Champions League
Who would like to play for a professional football team
And see the Camp Nou
Who shares his football, his ideas and his bones
Who is lightning quick, big and stong
Who is a resident of Largs
O'neil.

**Josh Gilmour (11)**
Largs Academy, Largs

# Isle Of Islay

I see incredible views all around,
Singing Sands is one of the very famous grounds,
Lonely woods full of animals and trees,
Exactly where I want to be.

Of all the Scottish isles, it is the best by far,
For the other isles haven't exceeded the standard bar.

In Islay, they are very fond of fishing,
Some of the grannies are more fond of knitting.

Lobsters and crabs are caught every day,
Although there's a lot to pay,
Yearly, the tourists rack up,
I know that by visiting Islay, I didn't mess up.

**Rohan Meechan (12)**
Largs Academy, Largs

# The Dragon's Quiet Mountain

The rocky mountain sighs a cold, harsh breath,
I ruffle my large, damaged wings
And overlook the cold winter horizon
With a watchful amber eye,
It's very lonesome on this mountain
With few birds passing by,
As lonely as I am,
I've lived here for centuries with little trouble,
The distant fur trees whistle and sway,
Sometimes loneliness is okay,
People just have to get used to it, just like I did,
I spend my long days watching the river flow
Or the odd bird fluttering by,
Up on my quiet mountain.

**Scarlett Walker (12)**
Largs Academy, Largs

# Keep Calm And Canter On

The wind in my mane
As I plough through the water
Galloping fast
As the day just gets hotter.

What a wonderful day
To be on the beach
With a saddle on my back
I let my spirits run free
Free as can be!

I feel very light
Even with a rider
Perched on my back.

As I trot on the soft sand
My rider talks to me
With encouraging words of kindness.

Now the sun has almost set
And my wonderful day has ended
But I know tomorrow
We will go on another adventure!

### Kate Maccalman (12)
Largs Academy, Largs

# The Sea

I am perfect
I am blue
A very pretty blue
I shine like the sun
I reflect the sun
People admire me
Like I admire them
I give them cold sea
I give them hot sea
But only if they're nice to me
I love people
People love me
We are one big happy family
Sticks and stones may splash a lot
But I don't care what people say
Because I will give them horrible me
I am light
I am dark
I can be high
I can be low
It just depends what mood I'm in
So let me be!

## Jessica Helen Langdon (11)
Largs Academy, Largs

# War

The air was velvet-black,
Tanks rolled past, gunshots were fired in the distance,
Corpses were lying all around me,
What had I done?
The war had been going on for years,
There was no escaping it,
Wherever I went, the war followed in my footsteps,
The war changed me,
I was once a young innocent boy,
Now look;
A monster
That had killed millions of people,
It was time for me to stop,
I made the decision to end my life,
I took my revolver to my head,
Then I pulled the trigger.

**Callum Stewart (11)**
Largs Academy, Largs

# A Crabby Day

Hi, my name is Crabby
And I am not happy
Some people could even say I'm crabby.

I want to go in the sea
But the queen says I'm just like a flea
And that is why I am crabby.

I am like no other species, don't you see?
So why does the queen think she's better than me?

My claws go *snippety-snip* and *snappety-snap*
*Clippety-clip* and *clappety-clap.*

I have nothing better to do
And that's why I'm crabby with you.

## Jackson Burleigh (11)
Largs Academy, Largs

# Why Me?

Here they come again
They are pointing and laughing at me
All I can think is, *why me?*
What have I done to deserve this?
My smile falls to the floor
I don't know what to do
I have no one
No friends
Should I run or will they catch me?
This is the worst time of my life
My body curls in on itself
I don't feel safe
I want to leave this school
I want to leave this country
This world doesn't like me
No one likes me
I don't like me
But why?

**Emma Mattheessens (12)**
Largs Academy, Largs

# The Phone

Hi, I am a phone
Yes, I am an iPhone
And I know you're probably thinking
*Painfully boring*
But not when you belong to Olivia Killjoy
Although, her constant selfies bore me
And her endless snapping kills
But it's the drama, oh the drama!
Boys, girls and teachers, none can be missed out
And her stupid acrylic nails
(That she thinks make her 100 times more sassy)
Are so long that she can't even work me
But she thinks it is worth it for Insta.

**Noah Graham (12)**
Largs Academy, Largs

# Václav Hladký

**V** áclav Hladký, I am a professional player for St Mirren
**Á** nd since I was a child I've wanted to be a goalie
**C** hasing the ball is like chasing your dreams, keep going until you get there
**L** earning to chase my dreams and help me not to give up
**A** nd not giving up helps me to chase my dreams
**V** ery difficult to keep going if you don't get it right, but that is what you have to do, so keep going and chase your dreams!

## Cameron Samuel Greenham (11)
Largs Academy, Largs

# Poachers

**P** oachers are killing all of my fellow animals.
**O** ut in the hot sun, it's like a hot tub.
**A** s they're all being killed, I'm wondering if that could be me.
**C** hasing them around just isn't right.
**H** aving animals extinct, there's no way for them to come back.
**E** nding up just lying there dead.
**R** emember, you're killing them, would you like that to be you?
**S** o just stop ruining our world.

**Cara Russell (11)**
Largs Academy, Largs

# My Heartbreak: Mike Wheeler

My name is Mike
I rode to Starcourt Mall on my bike

I saw Eleven at the mall
Her and Max looked like a doll

Then she dumped me
That really thumped me

Then she jumped on a bus
But she was in no rush

I tried to buy her a present
But it ended up being unpleasant

Now my heart has a hole
And my soul has to go

Mileven left the chat
Now I really need Dustin's cat.

**Ellie Smith (11)**
Largs Academy, Largs

# The Life Of The Overused Hoover

**H** ow come they always seem to need me? Like, how much mess do they make?
**O** ut, in, out and in all day long with pencils, rubbers, gum and more!
**O** h my god... Eww... What is that? And it's squishy, ew!
**V** ery gross... What do they even do?
**E** very hour, I get dragged out, and they never empty me!
**R** idiculous! That's what it is, it's almost like they don't even know I am alive!

**Ophelia Charlotte Elizabeth McNeill Conner (12)**
Largs Academy, Largs

# The Life Of Bread

I'm just a piece of bread,
My life, suddenly, hanging by a thread,
Trapped in this heat-cased prison,
I can hear my soul fizzin',
My whole existence is taken for granted,
I will start the biggest rant yet!
I can feel my skin hardening,
There's no point in bargaining,
Here comes the chocolate spread,
Seeing this fills me with dread,
Because now I know,
Humans are our greatest foe.

**Fraser Angus MacLean Waters (12)**
Largs Academy, Largs

# Can You Guess?

I hate when people open me wide
They watch, read and examine my inside

Carefully take in everything they see
And choosing whether or not to judge me

How dare they!
It makes me crazy!

These words in me tell a story
That could fill you with great glory

Can you guess what I am?
I bet you can

That's right, take a look
I am a book.

**Hannah McNicol (12)**
Largs Academy, Largs

# Jack The Lantern

Goodbye, Tom,
Goodbye, Jerry,
Right now, I'm not very merry.

People picking pumpkins gets worse every year,
But now it's my time to go, I fear.

Goodbye, field,
Goodbye, everything.

Wait, I'm alive, how can that be?
Feeling very joyful, sparkling with glee.

Now there's a light inside of me,
I can finally see!

## Strath Ferguson (12)
Largs Academy, Largs

# Garfield

**G** arfield is what they call me
**A** lways eating lasagne and sleeping is what I do
**R** olling around in bed all day long is what I do
**F** eeding me is Jon's job
**I** hate going to the vet
**E** ating Squeak the mouse is never an option for me
**L** asagne is the best thing to eat
**D** evouring lasagne is what I do.

**Rhys Joshua Franchetti (12)**
Largs Academy, Largs

# The Sassy Puppy

Okay, I have to say this
I am very mad at humans
They can be mean, and disgusting
But some humans are nice
Because they rub my belly
But some think I am smelly
Even though I have a bath every day
Well, in my muddy bath, I *hate* water!
Although most dogs love water
But I *hate* it...
Don't touch me, argh!

## Ava Miriam Barbour-Weatherill (11)
Largs Academy, Largs

# Superman

**S** imply amazing
**U** p here, looking down at the city
**P** ressing through the air
**E** xcited like a lion at a zebra festival
**R** amming bad guys, putting them in jail
**M** arrying Lois was probably the best part
**A** nd yes, if the bad guy has kryptonite, it hurts
**N** o, I don't regret being Superman.

## Cooper Wark (12)
Largs Academy, Largs

# The Lonely Can

**L** ying in the streets alone
**O** nly me, just me
**N** ever will I find a friend
**E** very day I'm kicked about
**L** onely and in pain
**Y** ou walk by and just ignore me

**C** an you be my friend?
**A** friend, a friend
**N** ow I feel much better with a friend.

## Frederick L F Smith (12)
Largs Academy, Largs

# Earth

**E** veryone is killing me
**A** fter multiple warnings, you are still littering
**R** ead the news and see my rainforest burning away
**T** he youth in twenty years will not know that trees existed
**H** elp save the world, not all heroes wear capes.

**Ruaridh Wightman (12)**
Largs Academy, Largs

# Through The Eyes Of Walt Disney

As I sit here
And look at the massive castle
Lights shining all over it
Fireworks bursting into the sky
I see people bursting into joy
Because of me
And I remember
It all started with a mouse.

### Victoria Cox (11)
Largs Academy, Largs

## Sheep Have Feelings Too

I am a sheep
As white as can be
And I am as fluffy as a bumblebee
But some people say I may have fleas
I live on a farm on the hillside
But sometimes it's cold and on the chill side!

### Freya MacArthur (12)
Largs Academy, Largs

# The Cruelty Of Hunting And Traps
*A haiku poem*

Hunting is so cruel
The traps clamp down on our paws
The humans made these.

### Rowan Guthrie Roberts (12)
Largs Academy, Largs

# Nagini

*A haiku poem*

I'm too shy to talk
Should stand up to Voldemort
I have to obey.

## Nitcha McLaughlin (11)
Largs Academy, Largs

# Just The Thought Of You

I can't think of anything better than a date
A gift like you would never come too soon
There's something I want to ask and I just cannot wait
For a gift like you I would fly to the moon.

I see a beautiful woman, under the stars you lie
Will you say yes? Now is the time to choose
Just to hear your voice, to the moon I would fly
I have no fear to ask it, I have nothing to lose.

Today, tomorrow and forever, you are the girl I'll miss
Together we will be complete, you know you have the power
I hope you know I truly love you, I just want a kiss
When it's time for you to leave I will give you more than a flower.

I know you will always wish you were my girl
Just the thought of losing you makes me want to hurl.

**Seif Elbadry (12)**
St Thomas More Catholic School, Bedford

# An Orphan's Sorrowful Life

Here I am, sitting in an orphanage
Wondering, *where is my mother and do I have a brother?*
I sit up from summer to winter
And it feels like I've had no dinner.

The noises of children having fun outside
Wake me up and make me want to cry
I think to myself, *what did I do wrong to my mother?*

When people give me clothing, I start to stutter,
I say to myself, *I want my mamma.*

Day and night, I look up to the light
Because it makes me wonder if my life will ever be alright.

I don't want the toys
I want the voice
For my mum to hear me from afar.

I feel traumatised when the carer ladies
Say that I don't have a mother
So why do I bother?

**Jessica Abisola Samuel (11)**
St Thomas More Catholic School, Bedford

# The Truth Of A Footballer

You ask about my prediction of the match,
In contrasts, and use lots of match facts.
You ask about my left foot,
As I give you my long practise input.
I take my essentials: ball, boots and kit,
To make sure I look fit.
Without care, I swish back my long black hair,
You look upon me with admiration,
I wonder if I will be a sensation.
I dribble, I run and I practise all night long,
As you encourage me along.
All match long, I quickly run and sneakily pass and shoot...
Not a goal!
All match long, you shout and scream.
All match long, I pass to my team.
All match long, I sweat and sweat,
But
One thing that really annoys me is
I never hit the net.

### Oisin Baird (11)
St Thomas More Catholic School, Bedford

# What Have I Done Wrong?

I was in court
When the judge shouted, "Guilty!"
I placed my head in my hands and sobbed
"But what have I done wrong?"

Two tough men carried me by the arms
My cell stank
Everyone thought I was a terrible person
What have I done wrong?

I couldn't sleep for nights on end
All bad things sprinting through my head
I struggled to eat
Nobody liked me
What have I done wrong?

I don't care about my death sentence
Or what the news is telling the world about me
All I care about is my family
They think I am horrible
They are being lied to
I need them to know I'm innocent
What have I done wrong?

**Eleanor Dutton (11)**
St Thomas More Catholic School, Bedford

# The Doctor

I don't want to go home
Locking the door and picking up the phone
I can't imagine their faces
Hearing the most terrible cases.

Telling someone a relative has died
I feel so bad that I just want to lie!
Telling someone that they have to say goodbye.

I can't take it!
I can't fake it!
It is impossible to say it!
Being the bearer of bad news
Saying the patient couldn't make it.

I want to crawl down a hole
Waiting for life to unfold
Wealth cannot heal my despair
For a patient of mine surviving is rare.

I just want to stop it all,
I don't want to ruin lives anymore...

## Ryan Ythan Grobates Apolinario (11)
St Thomas More Catholic School, Bedford

# An Actor's Life

I wake up in the morning and I practise my lines
You all think that I know them, but I improvise and mime.

I arrive on set and get ten cameras in my face,
Even though I'm at a completely different pace.

I have to practise with movies every day and night,
I find it hard expressing emotions like fright.

Interviews daily, questions piling up,
I don't think I can handle this, I might throw up.

I'm sitting on set with my hammer,
Watching myself beat up Bruce Banner.

I don't like that purple grape called Thanos, I should have gone for the head,
Now half the universe is dead!

## Luca Scozzari (11), Antonio Donny Bosco & Fintan Horsman
St Thomas More Catholic School, Bedford

# A Change Of Heart

The dreams I have of your sapphire eyes
Your presence is that of a royal
My mind, a vortex, when I see you cry
Tell me, how do I show you how I am loyal?

My passion for you burns like a fire
Don't say this love will never last
With you my happiness is never dire
I'll protect you in the future, present and past.

You are the one, my closest mate
I can't stop dreaming, you're my one and only
No one could have predicted this perfect fate
My heart beats fast when you hold me.

Actually, no, I love another girl
Your attitude makes me want to hurl!

**Lorenzo-Dane Dipasupil (12)**
St Thomas More Catholic School, Bedford

# The Suicidal Sniper

I go to bed every night,
Tears in my eyes,
Just wanting to die.
I don't want to kill but I have to,
It's against my will.
I wake up every morning,
People pay me to kill,
That's why I do it,
But money is becoming less amusing,
Especially when you have to kill a family.
It's hard, so is life,
Soon I will feel like ending it,
Along with my life,
Ending my suffering
And flying up high
Where the angels sing
To see my daughter, wife and mother,
One more time,
Every time I shut my eyes
I hope,
More and more
That I'll die.

## Marley Bulzis (11)
St Thomas More Catholic School, Bedford

# You

Every day, every night,
I will cry if you are not in my sight,
I miss you the second you walk away,
When you are not here, it is just a plain day,
I will always try to win you,
Even if it's the last thing I do,
Take my heart, I've pulled it out for you,
You are the water and I am the seed,
When I saw you, it was love at first sight,
If anyone steals you, I'll be there to fight,
When I gaze on you, you always look great,
How about we go on a date?
When you are in my sight, my heart screams,
I hope I see you again in my dreams.

## Pablo Dy (12)
St Thomas More Catholic School, Bedford

# My Love

Without you, my love
I feel our love is not real
Without you, I'm a lost dove
These are the things I truly feel

Without you, my love, I'm sad
My heart beats heavy in my chest
And without you, I'm crazy mad

My sorrows make me feel depressed
I need to know you will not leave
I can't go a day without you
All these things make me strive to believe...

Without you, my love, I am like a dove who hasn't flown
Without you, my love, I am not as fluffy as a cloud

I love you, my love.

## Shaun Osasu Osaghae (12)
St Thomas More Catholic School, Bedford

# An Orphan

**A** life like mine isn't as easy as you think
**N** othing to do all day, no pets, no siblings to share secrets with and no one ready to give you a hug

**O** utside you probably think we have a playground but we don't
**R** ats are what you find in your bedroom every night
**P** ea stew and mouldy pears are the only things they serve
**H** ands are never washed in the orphanage
**A** nts are everywhere in this place
**N** othing in the orphanage is good or fun, I wish I had a better life and wasn't an orphan!

## Magda Pernisco (11)
St Thomas More Catholic School, Bedford

# A Life For A Life

The straps weigh heavy on my shoulders
The gun is cold in my hand
I think of my wife and my children
They'll never understand

I know what I must do
Two shots and it's done
My wife and my children will be spared
But I'll never see the sun

I can see it all clearly in my head
The panic, the explosion, the red
It won't be painful, just quick
It'll all be over, I'll be dead

I arrive, this is it, time to die
I raise the gun and close my eyes
A life for a life.

**Orlagh Louise Brunning (11)**
St Thomas More Catholic School, Bedford

# Please, Oh Please

Please, please, all I need is a hug
You, my beautiful person, my love
Come sit with me and we can share a mug
You, the best, are beautiful, just like a dove
Come on you, please, I just need a cuddle
Don't worry, I won't tell any mean lies
It's fine, I won't get things in a muddle
You're an angel that flies
Come over here and give me that kiss
Let's go on a romantic date
It will be full of bliss
I can't wait!
I'm coming over soon
Maybe you and me could go to the moon...

## Honey-Leigh Williams (13)
St Thomas More Catholic School, Bedford

# A Hairdresser's Life

Spending hours and hours
Just to make people look good
Not worrying about myself
No food
No water
Nothing
Crying every night
Trying to keep out of daylight
Every day I try to make myself pretty
But nothing works
Dry hands
Stressed
Conscious of how I look
Never getting a break
People say about their amazing trips
But I just don't care
Can't bear to listen
Just want to go home
All alone
Nowhere to run
Nowhere to hide.

**Molly Bedingfield (11)**
St Thomas More Catholic School, Bedford

# A Palette Of Grey

People always like my paintings,
But don't understand why I don't use colour,
You see, the problem is,
I have achromatopsia,
I see the world in black and white,
No shades of blue or green,
Nobody can understand the pain that I have,
Nothing will ever cure my colour-blindness,
I yearn to see those beautiful colours,
All the shades that the rainbow has,
But at least I still have that wonderful skill
That made me all the black and white money I have.

**Wojciech Bronakowski (11)**
St Thomas More Catholic School, Bedford

# Tom Brady

I play for New England Patriots,
The pressure is immense,
If I miss the shot, the game could be lost
And I will forever be known as he who missed the shot.

If I break a bone, then there goes
My job, my house, my money,
My life as I know it!

The play of the game is coming,
If I miss, it's over,
My career is over,
My pay will be cut
And all that I will have is a single cup!

The play of the game is here,
What will happen?

## Shaun Marsh (11)
St Thomas More Catholic School, Bedford

# You Are...

I can think of nothing except you dear,
you act so loyal,
please never leave and disappear,
you are so royal.

You take care,
you give me hugs and kisses,
just like a teddy bear,
those hugs feel like a million wishes.

You make me as light as a feather,
you have my heart,
together forever and ever,
just like your art.

I can't think of anything except for your love,
you are the one I just can't stop thinking of.

**Simren Kaur (12)**
St Thomas More Catholic School, Bedford

# An Actor's Life

When she is about to go on stage,
She is always sick.
When she sees a crowd,
She has had enough of it.
"I wonder how to overcome my fears,
Oh, I don't know," she says in tears.
My, my, what an actor,
They could maybe even sack her!
Inside her she thinks she's a mouse,
Even though she owns the house.
She has a dog,
A sausage as long as a log.
The dog, the one for which she cared,
He can sense whenever she is scared.

## Sama Mohamed Saeed Ali (11)
St Thomas More Catholic School, Bedford

# A Basketball Player's Life

You ask for my basketball,
As I jump, run and fall.
I dribble through the defenders,
And past all the away players.
I take my essentials: Jordans, balls and home vest,
I want to make sure I look my best.
My coach shouts, "Get in position!"
I freeze cold in anticipation.
The crowd cheer and shout, I pounce. Wow!
When I shoot in the hoop, I saw, "Wow!"
When I looked at the score, we won!

## Harvey Chiarn (11)
St Thomas More Catholic School, Bedford

# The Football Life

A football
What to do with it?
I just want to watch and sit
The pressure is on
Confidence is gone
To win that cup
Lost your luck
The only thing
To go and win
The day is here
Just lose your fear
Go and get that ball
Just don't fall
What a foul!
No, don't growl!
Halfway up the pitch
He got a stitch
In the box
He scored a goal
He didn't lose his soul.

**Leo Valentine Barker (11)**
St Thomas More Catholic School, Bedford

# Footballers' Famous Lives

People think
My life is well off and comfortable
But it's not
I have to cope with racist abuse
Training
Training every day
Hate my life
Please let me retire
Injury
Thank god, now I will have no more football
For a month
Back from injury
Oh no
29 years, 30 years, 31 years
I hate the fans
I hate my manager
Finally
I
Retire
Forever.

## Bryan Chanpda (11)
St Thomas More Catholic School, Bedford

# The Truth Of An Actor

All my fans ask for my autograph,
And all I hate is my photograph.
All those actors who are a disgrace,
Oh Lord, don't let anyone take my place.
All those directors who go astray,
Each with punishment for every delay.
Oh great, here comes that director,
They've started to blind me with that projector.
Now I know what to play...
Wait, what? It's Friday!

**Iggy Shanthakumar (11)**
St Thomas More Catholic School, Bedford

# My Sunshine

You are loyal
You are royal
My love for you shines brightly blue
You make my day
With your joyful play
Your smile is happy
Your smile is snappy
Oh boy you are cute
When you play with your toys
Your nose is so soft
Just like a grizzly bear
I would pay any cost
To see you
And with your ears so floppy
You make everyone stare.

## Max Ellis Owen (12)
St Thomas More Catholic School, Bedford

# The Truth Of The Queen

I'm not just anyone
I knew this from young
There would be guards and cameras
From everywhere I sprung.

I didn't choose this
No one even gave me a choice
But I did have one
I would want to be ordinary and rejoice.

I may find my king
I may walk alone
But I am the Queen
To that title, well-grown.

### Nancy Finn (11)
St Thomas More Catholic School, Bedford

# The VSCO Girl

I'm a VSCO girl
In a VSCO world
Scrunchie-tastic
Don't mess with plastic
Scrunchies in my hair
Sksksk everywhere
Without plastic
The world's fantastic
Dropped my hydro flask
And i-oooop
Kankan backpacks
Wearing Birkenstocks
Drink with metal straws
Save the turtles
It's our nation!

## Rebecca (12) & Victoria Jelisaveta Kaczalek
St Thomas More Catholic School, Bedford

# Alone

Sat on the streets of London
Watching people day in, day out
I curl up in the corner
Waiting to be loved
Seeing all the happy children
Bouncing up and down
Makes me wish I had a family
Just like them
People pay no attention
People scrunch their noses
They act like they can't see me
What am I meant to do?

**Sophia Hope Witton (11)**
St Thomas More Catholic School, Bedford

# An Immigrant

I want to go home
I left my family and friends
To come here
I'm scared of this
I'm scared of the people
And the schools
They are all new
But a bad new
Which I don't want
I want my old life
But I can't have it anymore
I cry and pray
To go back to my normal life
In my country.

**Alex Silva (11)**
St Thomas More Catholic School, Bedford

# The Refugee

Alone,
No friends, no family,
Alone,
No food, no water,
Alone,
No hope left in this cruel world,
Alone,
A home is all I want in this evil world,
Alone,
Will I die?
Alone,
Or will I survive?
Alone,
Last chance to get a home,
Or will I be
Alone?

**David Hallsworth (11)**
St Thomas More Catholic School, Bedford

# A Sniper

The sniper was scared of blood
Always lying in the cold and messy mud
Covered in Greenland camo
With a 2.3x scope
Firing automatic ammo
In the forest, hiding in the trees
Looking out for enemies
But being scared of blood
Injured teammates were not his speciality!

**Johnny Farmer (11)**
St Thomas More Catholic School, Bedford

# The Sniper

Imagine every time you look through the scope
You have to kill
You pull the trigger
And see the now corpse fall to the ground

Imagine trying to sleep at night
But you keep thinking of that sight
And saying to yourself, "Was that right?"

**Szymon Jedrzejewski (11)**
St Thomas More Catholic School, Bedford

# Colourless Eyes

I produce endless masterpieces,
Yet I cannot see what makes the world.
I hope there is a way for me,
I want to know what the real world is.
The way I suffer for others' amazement,
I want to see colour,
All I want to see is colour.

## Fin Crofts (11)
St Thomas More Catholic School, Bedford

# An Orphan - Who Wants To Be Loved

I've been left all alone,
Left in a world revolved around phones,
No one cares about me,
Stop being rude,
I've made myself a target for bullies,
Sadness fills me every day,
All I want is some love...

**Alexander Gallagher (11)**
St Thomas More Catholic School, Bedford

# Animals

Animals are so helpless
Here and there, their bodies lie with plastic
It's as if plastic is a donation to us
But a poison to animals

Why are animals so depressed?
Never get a life of peace?
One gets eaten, another dies through our choices
When will they get a life of peace?

We need to stop this
We can't just stop taking care of them
We need to change
Us united can change the world

Animals are so helpless
Here and there, their bodies lie with plastic
It's as if plastic is a donation to us
But it's a poison to animals

Animals get sad and die
So next time
Don't cry,
But instead, learn and do differently next time

Come on, we can do this
Put our minds together
We can change the world
Us united can accomplish our responsibilities.

## Hushmeet Singh Nagpal (11)
The Matthew Arnold School, Staines Upon Thames

# My Cute Little Eds

I wish I could feel my hand holding yours,
Your soft lips next to mine
And you loving me back

You have this beautiful hair that's brighter than the stars,
Two hypnotic eyes that are sweeter than chocolate,
A smile that affects me more than time
And a personality that's crazier than this world.

But what I simply want to say is that I love you,
But not even these words are able to explain what I feel for you,
How you make me laugh even when I can't smile,
And you make me feel secure when I'm breaking inside.

But sadly, I can't tell you how I feel
As you only see me as a friend,
So I hide my love with humour and pride.

And now that you're gone, all I do is cry
'Cause I was not strong enough to save you
And even though I'm not with you...
I feel death inside too.

I'm sinking fast,
The very next day might be my last
'Cause my cute little Ed, without you,
The world is not worth my time.

Please, Eddie, my love, don't make me wait too long
'Cause this trash mouth's life means nothing without you.

## Laura Valentina Mantilla (14)
The Matthew Arnold School, Staines Upon Thames

# Turtle's Perspective

Do you know what I see?
Do you know the pain I go through?
My family are dying every day because of these humans.
They're horrible!
They are hurting my family.

What's my worst enemy?
Plastic.
Plastic is everywhere in my home.
Every day I see either fish or my family of turtles eating it.
My family are in danger.
My home is in danger.
The sealife is in danger.
I live in fear.
Us sealife don't know the difference between food or plastic.
I wake up in fear and think,
*Am I going to die today?*

My family are dying every day because of these humans.
They're horrible.
They're hurting my family.
Now tell me...
Do you know what I see?
Do you know the pain I go through?

**Kacey Rice (13)**
The Matthew Arnold School, Staines Upon Thames

# Jokes From A Joker

These cities are atrocities
All are sceptics, critics
This isn't cryptic, it's apocalyptic
I'm now immune,
I am apathetic, never empathetic.

My soul is open, it is certain
Once utopia
Now dystopia.

So difficult to ponder
How I once began a hero
Then to surrender and realise...
Whoa!

You're doing my undoing
It's now clear
For the love of God, don't peer
Behind these assumed curtains.

The show must go on
The crowd were faced upon
These imbeciles and criminals.

Perhaps the bad wasn't so bad after all
If it was not so, a downfall
Was bound for a clown
Like me
Then, free...?

## Nicolly Victoria Jeronimo (16)
The Matthew Arnold School, Staines Upon Thames

# Through The Owl's Eyes

The glistening waters rushed,
The bright rose leaves did fall,
The wind howled towards
The magical waterfall.
Birds tweeted and launched off their nests,
Swooped over the hills
And landed on treasure chests.
In my home up above,
In the treetops full of happiness and love,
I swooped down the tree
And hooted once or twice.
Down below my claws scrambled tiny, little mice.
Approaching what seemed like an enchanted magical tree,
All the animals came to this important festival meeting.
Pandas, tigers, leopards,
Lions, birds, chameleons,
Other amazing animals,
Here today in this amazing world!

## Emma Jones (13)
The Matthew Arnold School, Staines Upon Thames

# War Is Foul And Foul Is War!

*Bang! Bang! Bang!*
Bullets flying past my head,
A little peek and I am dead.
My brain aches in the merciless, cold east winds,
Sitting in the trenches, worried by silence and nervous.
Why do I feel like I'm gonna cry?
Is it because we will die?
Me and my friends
Are all of the same kind.
All three of us open fire,
I hear every sound as they rip through his life,
I see broad daylight on the other side...

Then I'm home on leave, but I blink and think.
His life in my bloody hands...
The reddest eyeballs filled with tears.
*Bang! Bang! Bang!*

## Krrish Parajiya (15)
The Matthew Arnold School, Staines Upon Thames

# But Not Mine

I don't have nightmares at night
I live amongst mine at home
Whilst doing lines, I'm dying inside
Other parents prepare lunches
In their kids they take pride
But not mine.

When he's gone, I dread him coming back
All the stress and all the worry makes the panic attack
Other parents are happy
But not mine.

I wish it could all go away
And we could be a good family
Because one day there will only be me...
Amongst all this evil, I try to shine
And some parents would recognise
But not mine.

### Jack Barber (15)
The Matthew Arnold School, Staines Upon Thames

# The Future Is Upon Them

The future is upon them
From what their parents left behind
Poverty, pollution
On their Earth they find
That nothing is perfect
Nothing is pristine
Streets, oceans
None of it is clean.

The future is upon them
And they don't know what to do
Help? Protest?
They don't have a clue
Should they stand up for what they believe in
And raise their voice?
Shout? Scream?
Do they even have a choice?

The future is upon them
And the clock is ticking fast...

## Rachel Jimenez (13)
The Matthew Arnold School, Staines Upon Thames

# Memories To Remember

The memories we forget are the memories we hold onto,
The day he went, the day he went,
The day a piece of my heart went,
Died in the battlefield, lost and forgotten.

The day he came home, the day my heart melted,
His little smile, the little checks,
The way he woke up crying in fear,
The way my heart felt, letting him go.

And at the funeral, gunshot, trumpets and people crying,
I look at the gravestone, crying on my knees.

Why my son?
Why the one thing I love and cherish?

**Alex Jennings (15)**
The Matthew Arnold School, Staines Upon Thames

# Through Their Eyes

I stare at the news in awe,
My mouth agape,
Watching the polar bears' habitats melt,
Some lying on the ice and won't awake.

Through their eyes, they're crying,
Crying in need of help,
Watching their loved ones fade away like dust,
All they can do is yelp.

There can be hope,
For these isolated creatures,
But our society is messing up,
Exploiting all of their features.

**Laine Beacham (13)**
The Matthew Arnold School, Staines Upon Thames

# Through The Eyes Of A Teenager

**M** ind is spinning
**E** very day is a struggle
**N** ew day? More like same day
**T** ougher and tougher it gets
**A** lways feeling down
**L** ooking at the ground

**H** elp I'm getting
**E** very day with a therapist
**A** t school with friends
**L** ost in confusion
**T** ired and in pain
**H** elp me please, before I lose my mind...

**Grace Ager (15)**
The Matthew Arnold School, Staines Upon Thames

# In The Wind

I love life and nature too,
I really like it here with you!
You get to climb on me in summer,
Until you fall... what a bummer!
You like it here, you really do,
And no one says that I don't too!
I really like it in the spring,
When I can blossom in the wind!
I'm a tree - and you can't live without me!

## Luca Saftoiu (11)
The Matthew Arnold School, Staines Upon Thames

# The Chewing Death

As I live,
You set me free,
Then you make me
You make me die.
If you love me,
Then keep me alive,
But if you hate me,
Then kill me.
I need a rest,
Please don't eat me!
Keep me alive,
I'm alone,
I have no friend,
Please help.
Keep me,
Love me.

## Sarah Abusaid (11)
The Matthew Arnold School, Staines Upon Thames

# Through Their Eyes

Through their eyes, they think it's okay,
To stop and laugh at people all day.
Through their eyes, all they think,
Is the people that they laugh at are weak.

He's too scared to talk,
Too scared to speak out,
Too scared to talk to his parents,
Too scared they'll shout...

## Luke Francis (13)
The Matthew Arnold School, Staines Upon Thames

# Buzz, Buzz

*Buzz! Buzz!* I'm a black and yellow bee
I'm hiding in places you can't even see
The world is catching up to me
Hour after hour, another one dies
But nobody will ever hear my little bee cries
I'm hiding and camping in my hive
If I leave, will I come back alive?

## Alfie Bailey (15)
The Matthew Arnold School, Staines Upon Thames

# Boris Johnson's Brexit

**B** oris is our lord and saviour
**R** eally means everything to everyone
**E** xiting the European Union was his greatest plan but
**X** enophobia is not okay
**I** t really shouldn't be the way
**T** herefore I don't agree with this, but I do agree with Brexit.

## Mathew Foster (15)
The Matthew Arnold School, Staines Upon Thames

# Crooks

This poor man is out of luck,
And has become a stable buck,
Sleeping in a box of straw,
Better than living on the floor.

He used to have the American dream,
Gone are the days full of gleam,
Who knows why no one would care,
It seems that no one was aware.

**George Bignell (13)**
The Matthew Arnold School, Staines Upon Thames

# The Zombies

The zombies
They're coming
They're *coming!*
Creeping down the halls
Are a herd of ghostly ghouls
They scatter and scram
As they approach you, you run and scream
All you do is pretend it's a dream...

**Oliver Long (11)**
The Matthew Arnold School, Staines Upon Thames

# Boris, Boris

Boris, Boris, get your Rolex and flex it
Boris, Boris, let's crack on with Brexit
Theresa said she can see you
Let's just leave the EU
The Queen is agreeing with me
So fly like a butterfly and sting like a bee.

## Louis Reed (15)
The Matthew Arnold School, Staines Upon Thames

# War

**W** ent onto the field
**A** djusted my gun
**R** est in peace to the soldier who's done nothing wrong.

## Heston Charles Reed (15)
The Matthew Arnold School, Staines Upon Thames

# 1... 2... 3, The End Of Me

I walk into school, all eyes on me,
I go home alone, sad, but no one ever sees.
They kick and punch me until I cry,
Then they leave me alone and I just want to die.
The notes are the hardest,
Though people think they are harmless.
'Kill yourself, hurt yourself'.
I think, *why would I do that to myself?*
Then I look in the mirror
And I just look so queer.
I wonder why,
Why they want me to die.
In the dark alone,
Too scared to look at my own phone.
It pings and pings,
Not because people want to speak,
But because they know I am weak.
I go back fighting strong,
But the day drags on for too long.
Long enough for me to fall apart,
Please, someone, just let me restart.
Every day it's the same old home
But to me, it's a big dark dome.
I see my brother, Lee,
I think, *does he even love me?*
No, no one does, do they?

There's always a new day,
But if only there was a new life.
I could end this one with a knife.
I wish it didn't have to end like this,
I wish I could give my family one last kiss.
Love you Mum, love you Dad, and I love you Lee,
1... 2... 3...

## Summer Henning (12)
Upton Hall School FCJ, Upton

# What Do You See When You Look At Me?

What do you see when you look at me?

I am an eighty-seven-year-old woman, a widow, a mother of three
Who is very lonely.
You see an old lady who moves slow,
As I haven't got anywhere to go.

My hair is silver in colour, my face is wrinkled too,
I can't remember my name or what I needed to do.

You look at me like I've lost my marbles,
But really I have just lost my sparkle.
I hate how everyone treats me like a fragile rose
And makes a fuss when I need to cross the road

I nursed the sick in the war,
But now I am not so quick anymore.
You rush past, knocking me out the way,
Do you know I won two running medals in my day?

Do you care to know?
Can you look a bit deeper and see
I am not a crazy old woman,
I am Mary,
A widow,
A mother,

An athlete,
A nurse.

Come and sit down, let's have some tea,
Listen and I'll tell you all about me...

**Ava Langley (11)**
Upton Hall School FCJ, Upton

# Who Am I?

I am a young woman,
Twenty-two,
An adult.
My life is different,
I was shot.
Shot for standing up for girls' rights.
Ridiculous, right?

The Taliban,
They ripped apart our beautiful valley
And stopped girls going to school.
I didn't want to stop going to school,
So I protested.
Life was unfair,
Life *is* unfair.
Waking up to screaming and explosions,
Scared to never leave your bed,
God your only comfort.
Guess what?
You won't believe this,
They even banned television.
I ignored this!

Silence,
That's what they wanted.
To silence me.

Shut me up.
So they shot me.

Life is a road,
It changes.
That's how I ended up here,
In Birmingham - after recovering from my wounds.
I won't give up,
I will fight for those in Pakistan.
I am Malala.

### Hannah Brearton (11)
Upton Hall School FCJ, Upton

# Minority

When I was a child,
I had no one at school.
When I was a child,
I was laughed at by other kids.
When I was a child,
People only spoke to me if they were being mean.
When I was a child,
It was harder than I could handle.

Every day,
I felt less included, included in the community.
Every day,
There was someone new, someone who felt they could treat me unfairly.
Every day,
Someone turned away, away from me.
Every day,
I looked around and saw nothing but people, people who didn't understand.

Now,
I have people to go to.
Now,
I laugh with my friends.
Now,
People have conversations with me.

Now,
I can handle my new life.

Now,
I am appreciated in the community.
Now,
I am treated fairly.
Now,
People come towards me.
Now,
People understand.

And so do I.

**Bethany Addenbrooke (11)**
Upton Hall School FCJ, Upton

# A Name

What does it mean,
This simple name?
A word in Greek, German or Latin?
Am I named after my personality?
Maybe?
I doubt it.
But what could my name be?

"It's just a name," you might say,
Of course, I know that.
But what I want to know is what does it mean?
Is it the name for a goddess?
A word meaning 'cow'?
Is it an insult?
What does it mean?

I am an English girl with a German name.
My name means hard-working
And so I know why it suits me.
I worked hard for answers
And now, I have found them.

I have no more questions,
They have all been answered,
Each and every one.
Now that I have no more questions,
What should I do?

My name is Emily.
So who are you?

## Emily Grace Lowry-Bartram (11)
Upton Hall School FCJ, Upton

# Annoying Brothers!

A tough life for me, a cross I have to bear
Poor me, burdened with two little tearaways
One called Alfie, one called Frankie
Life with them sure makes me cranky!

They don't have to do a single thing wrong to make me explode
A knock on my door
A pull of my hair
A smug little grin
Just thinking of it makes me want to implode!

Stealing my stuff
Taking over the PS4
All starts a war
Trying to take my turn, they lock the door
Oh Mother, help me ditch this crazy pair!

If only Mum and Dad took heed and gave me a baby sister
My life would have been so much simpler, I know I couldn't resist her
Instead, for now, I'll grin and bear it
But to be legit
I need to admit
I love them dearly!

### Annelie Wheeler (11)
Upton Hall School FCJ, Upton

# I'm Sorry...

Bullying makes me feel unhappy,
The way they act is just so bratty.
Threatening, making me keep my lips sealed,
Nobody understands how I feel.
Putting bad thoughts inside of my head,
I can just tell that I'm wanted dead.
I dread waking up every day in the morning,
I come home from school and I can't stop bawling.
My parents always question all the bruises on my skin,
I tell them, "I'm just clumsy, walked into the bin."
They ask me if my day was good, I don't know what to say,
Floods of tears inside my eyes, I say it was okay.
How can I tell my parents all the mean things they said?
What if they wake up one morning and find me dead?
I'm sorry, Mum,
I'm sorry, Dad,
I love you...

**Karen Kiama (12)**
Upton Hall School FCJ, Upton

# I Can't Get Out

In the dismal woods,
Isolated and lonely,
Quiet whispers of wind,
Icy chills filled my body,
Now trapped in a nightmare
And I can't get out!

Blankets of leaves
At my toes,
Camouflaged animals growling,
Now my foes.

Voice shivering,
Words stuttering,
Now trapped in a nightmare
And I can't get out!

A blinding light,
A blood-clotting cold,
An electric scream
And a cry pure and bold.
Torture...
Now I'm trapped in a nightmare
And I can't get out!

Footsteps approaching,
Chasing me,
Branches clattering,

But it can't be...
Now trapped in a nightmare
And I can't get out!

## Emma Harrison (12)
Upton Hall School FCJ, Upton

# Landlock

Landlock all by himself,
*I have not seen my family in months,*
What has happened?

Landlock sees birds,
Must stay away,
Don't want to be lunch.

Landlock hears dolphins,
Dolphins aren't nice,
Stay clear of them!

Landlock encounters boats, lots of boats,
Fish on boats, don't move,
Must be careful.

Landlock sees fish, same type of fish as him,
He wants to follow them,
They lead him into a crack and into the sea.

They lead him to his family,
They're as happy as can be.

He's not Landlock anymore,
He's salmon,
Like his family.

**Sasha Ratchford (11)**
Upton Hall School FCJ, Upton

# Teen Life

Being a teen
Oh, it's tough
Read this poem
You'll learn, it's rough.

Instagram, Facebook, Snapchat
All we get is chat, chat, chat,
Gossip, gossip, gossip.
Everyone should just stop it.

Body-shaming! Oh, it's cruel.
Doing it does not make you cool.
It just makes you look mean,
Sitting there behind your screen.

Friends, friends - sometimes they're kind,
Sometimes they need to make up their mind.
Fun times are good, bad times are bad,
Don't take it to heart, don't be sad.

Being a teen - sometimes it's good,
But sometimes you want to put up your hood.

## Mollie Wilson (12)
Upton Hall School FCJ, Upton

# Bullying

Bullying has got to stop
Before it goes over the top.
People start to cry through the day,
"Why won't this just go away?"

*Bully's point of view:*
I feel so bad
That I made someone sad,
I regret everything I've done,
Now bullying's not so fun.

*Victim's point of view:*
They verbally abuse me and leave me all alone,
Sometimes I wish I could just stay at home.
The words they say to me
Really hurt me,
The words they say to me
Really kill me.
I sometimes wish that I could just be free,
Escape from this life and just be me.

**Phoebe Ferguson (13)**
Upton Hall School FCJ, Upton

# Dear Diary

All of these thoughts are running and yelling in my head,
Screaming and screeching, trying to escape.
You're probably wondering many things, like...

Where are my parents?
What do you mean?
Why do you feel this way?

My parents don't love me!
No one loves me...

I dream every night of a better place,
Like living in a hut, on a beach of a tropical island,
Where fruits grow, birds sing and trees flourish.

A place where everyone will love me.
A place where everyone is equal.
A place like Heaven.

I'll see you soon.
- Written on the day I died.

## Amelia Hennell (12)
Upton Hall School FCJ, Upton

# The Earth Isn't On Fire

The Earth isn't on fire,
At least that's what they say,
The turtles are wearing
Necklaces of plastic
And the trees are cast away.

The Earth isn't on fire,
The companies plead,
All the deforestation
Is for all their wealth and greed.

The Earth isn't on fire,
Well, that's what people shout,
As the ice is melting
And the deserts are heating,
And the animals have no way out.

The world is on fire
And the deforestation is getting worse.
All of our animals are going extinct,
So let's stop before we can't reverse it.

**Lucy Turner (12)**
Upton Hall School FCJ, Upton

# Friends

Ever since I moved,
All my friends have been mean to me.
They never invite me to parties
And don't ask me round for tea.

It makes me feel really sad
And for some reason, they don't feel bad.
They don't understand how upset I get,
All because of them.

They say mean things about me, behind my back and to my face.
If I could, I'd put them in a rocket
And blast them off to space!

It's been a whole year now since I've seen my 'friends',
I think I'm getting over it
But they still get on my nerves a bit.

## Neve Piercy (11)
Upton Hall School FCJ, Upton

# Take A Chance

A bead of sweat,
An eerie feeling,
A chill down my spine,
The burden of life;
Who would trust me?

That vast darkness
Looming over me,
Taunting me;
"What are you worth?"
An unanswerable question.

Every rose has its thorns,
Not worth the pain
For the potential beauty;
Who would risk that?

Wherever I turn,
Whatever I do,
The wall only gets higher;
Not that I'd try to climb.

A hope on top,
Too high to reach,
You can only change
If you take a chance;
Not a bad idea...

**Imogen Hunt (11)**
Upton Hall School FCJ, Upton

# Help!

My home is gone
Burned down by the people -
The ones that want money.
They don't care about the consequences,
Just blinded by what they want.
They value these things
More than the world we live in.

We need help,
But no one listens to us,
We're just the pesky creatures
In the way of their 'big ideas'.
They think everything is fine,
But they don't know the truth.
What is happening?

I just want it to stop,
Before it's too late
And we can't do anything to stop it.

## Mia Annabel Waring-Jones (12)
Upton Hall School FCJ, Upton

# I Am Summer

My name is Summer,
I come after spring,
I admire all the flowers
And hear the birds sing.

The sun shines brightly,
Throughout the wood,
With luscious greenery,
It feels like a flood.

The tides come briskly,
Then run away,
The waves crash loudly,
Then vanish all day.

The blue skies and sunshine
And the odd drop of rain,
The colours are vibrant
Down the hot country lanes.

I hide in the winter,
As cold's not my thing.
My name is Summer,
I come after spring.

**Lucy Birtwistle (11)**
Upton Hall School FCJ, Upton

# It's Not Fair

I can't become a doctor,
Or help animals as a vet,
I want to be a scientist
But I can't, not yet.

What am I supposed to do?
What career is there for me?
I don't want to be a maid,
It's not fair - there's no equality.

He can become a doctor,
Or help animals as a vet,
He wants to become a scientist,
And *he* can, I bet.

My brother can go to school,
He learns all about the world,
I don't have that opportunity,
Because I'm a girl!

**Emily May Jackson (11)**
Upton Hall School FCJ, Upton

# Injustice

I sat...
Alone.
Filled with the rage of injustice.

The court thought I was guilty.
"The murder of Thomson Smith."
I plead innocence, of course.
I thought I was one step ahead,

Turns out I'm a step behind.

They're just not listening.
They don't understand.

These 'things' were not created by God,
But the Devil himself.

Invading our lives like
The rats in the Plague.

Let's just say, I'm cleaning the streets...

**Madelyn McGreevy (12)**
Upton Hall School FCJ, Upton

# The Old Lady's Memories

In my chair I lay,
As I watch the children come out to play,
Remembering the day
When my friends used to say,
"Wanna play out today?"

We used to play with skipping ropes,
Whilst talking about our dreams and hopes.
Then we would make rose petal soaps,
In-between the mesmerising old oaks.

We didn't just play in the warm months though,
We also played when the leaves began to blow,
And even when it started to snow.
And at the end of the day, we would all be sad to go.

**Dakota Drake (12)**
Upton Hall School FCJ, Upton

# My Life

Trapped,
A world with no escape.
The laughs, the mockery,
It makes my heart ache.

My reputation has been destroyed,
And I am broken.
The further they go,
The deeper it tortures me.
The more they go,
The deeper it kills me.

The words are upsetting,
Yet I'm letting
Them ruin
My life.

But I see a light,
A glowing hope.
My emotions are rewired,
One step at a time.

I am gaining
Happiness and joy,
As I rebuild
My life.

**Amy Mair Flanders (12)**
Upton Hall School FCJ, Upton

# Rabbits Aren't Made For Mascara

Rabbits aren't made for mascara,
We aren't meant for blush either!
We used to be grazing around
Now my home's a science lab.
It's not so nice in here,
I wish it was over,
I wish it would disappear.
I am already blind in one eye,
It hurts to cry,
My skin is itchy and irritated,
I want to die.

Rabbits aren't made for mascara,
We aren't made for blush either!
Make sure to look for cruelty-free,
It might not be easiest for you
But it saves me.

**Hollie Cowen (13)**
Upton Hall School FCJ, Upton

# Superheroes

I've always aspired to be
One of the superheroes who protect New York City.
There's Spider-Man and his awesome sticky webs,
Superman, who flies across the sky in his bright red cape,
Batman, with his solid, cast-iron fists,
Iron Man with his ultimate mechanical suit,
Captain America and his supreme metal shield,
Thor and his huge, almighty hammer,
And Black Widow with her formidable martial arts.
All of these superheroes I dream to be,
But the only superhero I can really be is me.

**Rowan Swale-Beswick (11)**
Upton Hall School FCJ, Upton

# They Are Dying

Red, orange, yellow
Are the colours I see every day,
My cousins, sisters and brothers
Slowly fade away...

The trees are falling down,
The trees are falling down, they say,
But the more and more they seem to decay,
I sometimes wonder, *will it ever stop?*
But they still seem to drop.

To raise awareness for this cause,
We all need to help and put it on pause,
To stop it before it's too late,
Before we all have a terrible fate.

Save the Amazon!

**Lili-Louise Amis (11)**
Upton Hall School FCJ, Upton

# Imprisoned

I stand still in my prison
Which could take my life with a click of its fingers.

Lines upon lines of empty-faced Jews
Wait for their fate.

The anger builds inside every one of us
As we stand tall in our yellow stars.

The screams of children as they enter the chamber which could bring death,
Sends shudders down your back.

Your legs shake beneath you
As you make your way to the front of the queue.

Life or death?
Only he will decide...

**Mae Evie Hodgers (12)**
Upton Hall School FCJ, Upton

# Remember We're Here

The smell of injustice
The taste of fear
As I watch from my window
Deathly screams take my ear
Can anybody hear us?
Remember we're here.

Are we forgotten?
When will help appear?
Every day we question
Is the end near?
Every day I question
Is it worth living in fear?

Will there ever be freedom?
The future's unclear
If we all stand together
Will the hate disappear?
We know you can hear us -
Remember we're here...

**Anna Ryan (12)**
Upton Hall School FCJ, Upton

# My Silent Cry

The smell of fire burning around me,
Baby animals wandering around, looking for their mummy.
Buzzing machines flying above me,
Taking photos of this monstrosity.
My silent cry echoing through the atmosphere,
Hoping help is somewhere near.
The Amazon animals running away,
From the boiling hot fire coming my way.
My forest family falling to the floor,
My turn next; I am at death's door...

How hard it is to be me,
A silent, suffering South American tree.

### Millie Ellen Newton (11)
Upton Hall School FCJ, Upton

# Don't Stop!

Keep going until you're at the top
Don't stop, stop, stop!

Have courage and faith
Be great, great, great!

Be happy and healthy
Be alive, alive, alive!

Have a smile and a style
Be wild, wild, wild!

Be you and you only
Don't change, change, change!

As the world will come falling down.
If you're all the same, it's boring!

Have peace and a good heart
Then nothing will be bad, sad or set apart!

## Gia Hothersall (13)
Upton Hall School FCJ, Upton

# Plastic Pollution

Plastic packaging
Polluting the Earth
Our future
Must be sustainable
We can do it
It is attainable
Save the oceans and seas
Listen to our pleas
Shopping bags, bottles and drinking straws
Deadly pollution
Plastic is the cause
Killing creatures
Killing the Earth
We must save it
The land of our birth
We must start now
You must see
We can save our planet
It starts with you and me.

(Now read from bottom to top)

## Grace Stella Harvey (11)
Upton Hall School FCJ, Upton

# Marmite

Yum... Eww...
Some people like the way I taste,
Some people think I stink.
Why can't I be like jam?
Then no one would throw me down the sink.
For some, I make their mouths water,
Others, their tongues roll, *Irr,*
Others just can't bear my taste.
Some say I smell like a troll.
Smothered on a buttery crumpet,
A kick to cheese on toast,
A warm bedtime drink,
A midnight snack.
Whatever it is -
I'm loved or hated the most!

**Evelyn Gallon (12)**
Upton Hall School FCJ, Upton

# Change The World

I want to change the world,
To help those who need it,
For everything to become equal.

I can change the world,
Stand up to our oppressors.

I refuse to let them bring us down,
Or to tell us what to do,
We will make our own history,
We will not be made to stand, nor queue.

I had a dream
Where our Earth was right and just,
I want to make a difference,
To be someone you can trust.

I will change the world!

## Lara Corcoran (11)
Upton Hall School FCJ, Upton

# Living Behind A Screen

Why is it called social
When you're living behind a screen?
People being bullied and people being mean.
Don't be to him, her or me!

Instagram, Snapchat and Facebook,
Go into the kitchen and cook,
Or go into the corner and read a book.
Don't waste your time behind a screen,
Where people can be so mean.
Why is it called social
When you're living behind a screen?

**Rosie Beamish (12)**
Upton Hall School FCJ, Upton

# I Am The Music

It fills my body and helps me fly.
It takes me on a journey to faraway places.
It is the place I go to when I am lonely.
It holds me in the arms of its rhythm and sends me to sleep.

It falls like water over me and calms me.
It feeds me with its deep melodies.
It colours my mind as it dances in my head.

I am the music,
I will never turn it down.

**Faye Simpson (11)**
Upton Hall School FCJ, Upton

# Me!

I am young,
I am healthy,
But
I am not safe.
We live in Africa
In a small house,
Mice are scattering about.
I don't go to school,
I don't have friends,
I am alone!
I am starving, thirsty and overwhelmed
By this journey of torture.

Someone find me...

**Harriet Andrews (12)**
Upton Hall School FCJ, Upton

# We All Start Somewhere

The beginning,
The stress, the anger, the tears,
The falls, the injuries, the setbacks.
The middle,
The dreams, the goals, the hard work.
The end result,
The awards, the fame, the glory.

We all start somewhere.

**Kate Farmer (12)**
Upton Hall School FCJ, Upton

# YOUNG WRITERS INFORMATION

We hope you have enjoyed reading this book – and that you will continue to in the coming years.

If you're a young writer who enjoys reading and creative writing, or the parent of an enthusiastic poet or story writer, do visit our website www.youngwriters.co.uk. Here you will find free competitions, workshops and games, as well as recommended reads, a poetry glossary and our blog. There's lots to keep budding writers motivated to write!

If you would like to order further copies of this book, or any of our other titles, then please give us a call or order via your online account.

Young Writers
Remus House
Coltsfoot Drive
Peterborough
PE2 9BF
(01733) 890066
info@youngwriters.co.uk

Join in the conversation!
Tips, news, giveaways and much more!

YoungWritersUK    @YoungWritersCW